Books by Grace Langdon and Irving W. Stout
Published by The John Day Company

TEACHING MORAL AND SPIRITUAL VALUES

BRINGING UP CHILDREN

THE DISCIPLINE OF WELL-ADJUSTED CHILDREN

THESE WELL-ADJUSTED CHILDREN

By Grace Langdon

HOME GUIDANCE FOR YOUNG CHILDREN

TEACHING MORAL

AND SPIRITUAL

VALUES

A Parents' Guide to Developing Character

GRACE LANGDON, PH.D.

AND

IRVING W. STOUT, ED.D.

THE JOHN DAY COMPANY, NEW YORK

The John Day Company, 257 Park Avenue South, New York, N.Y. 10010 an Intext publisher

Published on the same day in Canada by Longmans Canada Limited.

Library of Congress Catalogue Card Number: 62-10949

Manufactured in the United States of America

FIFTH IMPRESSION

CONTENTS

TEACHING MORAL

AND SPIRITUAL VALUES

FOREWORD

IN THE BRINGING UP OF CHILDREN nothing can equal in importance the spiritual and moral values taught by parents at home as a guide to living.

Throughout the centuries of recorded history, both secular and sacred, it is plainly evident that when the individuals of a nation have turned predominantly to materialistic values then has come the decadence of that nation through the weakening of the moral fiber of the individuals in it. Any nation is strong only as the individuals comprising it are strong. Those individuals are strong only as their moral fiber is strong. Their moral fiber is strong only as they hold to fine, true standards of living.

The Founding Fathers of this nation held high their

9

belief in spiritual values as its reason for being. They set forth that belief in the opening lines of the Declaration of Independence when they wrote, "We hold these truths to be self-evident, that all men are created equal, that they are endowed by their Creator with certain unalienable Rights, that among these are Life, Liberty and the pursuit of Happiness." The very freedom and independence under which we live today stem from that recognition of spiritual values which they believed worthy of sacrifice.

We stand today before all the world openly and avowedly dedicated to those values which they set forth. Our dedication is reiterated on every piece of currency that passes through our hands in the words IN GOD WE TRUST. It is spoken each time the Pledge of Allegiance to our flag is repeated as we say, "One nation under God indivisible with Liberty and Justice for all." If our children today and in the days to come are to realize to the full their inimitable heritage, they too must have spiritual values by which to live. In no other way can they gather to themselves the happiness the pursuit of which is set forth as their inalienable right. Materialistic values alone have never sufficed to bring any lasting happiness. They will not now suffice.

It is in fine, true spiritual and moral values that strong, sturdy character has its roots. Those values lived *are* character. They furnish the standard for behavior. They are the guide to the choices any child is making hourly of what to do and not to do. They are the means by which he determines whether those choices are worthy and wise. They are a steadying force when temptations come. They ever shine as a light in a child's thought showing the true, right, honorable way to walk.

Here lies the answer to the query heard on every hand: "What can be done to prevent juvenile delinquency?" The answer lies in the teaching of spiritual and moral values at home and in helping a child to learn to love them and to live them. This is the only sure preventive of juvenile delinquency. When thought is filled with the true and good, there is no room in it for the wrong. Thought so filled has nothing in it upon which the suggestions of delinquent behavior can take hold.

A child lays hold readily upon the things of spirit. It is easy for him to look beyond the seen to the unseen. His thought is unhampered, untrammeled, free to soar. He wonders and questions, "What's behind the sky?" "What holds the stars up there?" "Who made the moon?" "Who made everybody?" "Who made the very first thing that ever was made?" Thus he seeks, as mankind has ever sought, to find the answer to man's existence and to the creation of the world. He reaches out, as mankind has ever reached out, for the eternal truths that have endured throughout all time under all conditions and that come into view in the spiritual and moral values we uphold.

A child easily accepts the idea of God as Spirit, as Creator of the universe, as the Giver of all good, as a loving, protecting Divine Power. He grasps without effort the idea of man's spiritual nature. The spiritual and moral values one would teach find ready lodgment in his thought as parents talk with him about being honest, courageous, gentle, truthful, loving, kind, generous, dependable; about doing to others as he would have them do to him.

Spiritual and moral qualities brought to sight in the activities of daily living are the natural expression of spiritual and moral values held in thought. Having their source in spiritual thought, they have a sure foundation. Unless they do come out of spiritual and moral values, they are empty of all that gives them meaning and sincerity. They are the letter without the spirit. Parents do well then to be ever sure that any quality of character which they would teach grows out of the thought which is its rightful source. Thoughts are ever the wellsprings of *action*.

Spiritual and moral values taught to a child from infancy on, coupled with the qualities that rightly express them, give him strength of character, nobility of purpose, and the only sure basis for deep and lasting happiness. Both values and qualities must be taught. A child cannot be expected to come upon them with surety and certainty otherwise. Each day brings its manifold opportunities for doing it in little practical ways. It is a word here, another there about the right and wrong of things; the little talks together about the ways of settling a difficulty; the pointing out that here is a way to put some value talked over before into action.

It is not always easy, indeed it is often difficult, to put into words for a child or even to formulate in one's own thought the exact nature of the values one feels it is the most important for him to grasp. Honesty, yes, but of what is honesty made? Truthfulness, surely, but what are the component parts of truthfulness? These a child must have help in knowing, if he is to live them. What are the thoughts to which one holds in order to be honest? truthful? generous? loving?

Many of the thoughts and feelings inherent in one intertwine with those of another. Thus courage whether it be physical or moral has in it bravery, valor, a willingness to meet a difficulty rather than evading it, and steadfastness that holds one to it though fear may suggest an easier way out. Honesty in its turn has courage in it, courage to deal fairly and squarely though there be the temptation to do otherwise.

The component parts of any spiritual and moral quality one may name intertwine with those of others, weaving together the whole fabric of character. Helping a child to see the separate details of each quality and to see how each relates to the other brings meaning to him far beyond any that can come when one says only, "I want you always to be an honest boy or girl." Or, "You know, dear, we must always be generous."

Nor is it enough to help him to see the aspects of the qualities one would have him learn. It yet remains to help him to see how to live them. Only then can his living show that consistency which is in itself a spiritual quality.

It was this that a mother was doing when she talked with her eight-year-old about the ball game with friends which had ended in a quarrel with charges hurled at him, "You didn't play fair—he wasn't out."
" 'Taint so, he wasn't either out "

"You want to be honest, don't you, dear?" she asked. "Yes," he sniffled, "but I was. I thought he was out." "Think it all over again," she said. "Are you sure you really thought so? Think where he was and where you were." "Well," he finally said, "I was almost there—I would'a been if I hadn't of slipped a little." •

The honesty and truthfulness which mother and boy had often talked about before had a little more mean-

14

ing to him because of that ball game difficulty. Courage came into the picture too, courage to admit that he had been wrong, courage to promise, "I'll play fair if you'll let me be first baseman again." The tiny bit learned that day added to other bits learned on other days will establish honesty as a spiritual value in thought and bring it more and more surely into the child's living. It is thus that character unfolds.

Difficult as it may be and often is to define for a child those values in which one most deeply and sincerely believes, it is needful to do so. Home is the place for a child to learn them. Parents are the ones to teach them. Only they can know the ones they would have their child to hold. It is they and they only who can give those early first teachings that are so potent; potent because they come first, potent because they are woven into thought with all the warmth of love, affection and care that parents give who truly love their child.

Even before a child understands the words that parents say, the things which they do and the way of doing them bring to him the values in which they believe. Their tenderness with him, their gentleness, their thoughtfulness for his well-being, are spiritual qualities which they themselves are putting into action. Everything said and done in the home bespeaks the values the parents hold. Let no one ever underestimate the importance of the teachings that go on there. As a child grows and goes out from home to school, to church, into the community, the values of others touch his living and have their influence. It is only at home though that they are interwoven with every detail of living—day to day, week to week, year to year— and with the closeness of the parent-child relationship.

Parents, the responsibility for teaching spiritual and moral values to your children is yours. No one can do it for you. Others can help but what they do is only supplementary to what you do. Much as they may love the child and great though their concern may be, they cannot have the relationship and influence which are yours by right of being parents. It is your responsibility and your privilege—a priceless one. It is the greatest gift you can give to your children.

With spiritual discernment you can see those values as parents through all the ages have seen them. Together with your child you can look deeply into those things which are the reflection of Spirit and which go far beyond anything reached through human reasoning. As you too hold to them even as you would have your child to do, your example as well as your precept will aid his learning.

None can say for another what values shall be taught nor how the teaching shall be done. The revealing of spiritual truths comes to different individuals in different ways at different times. Parents can bring those truths to a child only as they unfold to them in thought, but to anyone who reaches out with sincerity for them they come in some form. Those who understand and acknowledge God as the Creator of all good will naturally turn their children to Him as the source of the truths they teach. Those who are still searching for an explanation of existence and its purpose will bring spiritual truths to their children as they come to them. Thus learning goes on for both children and parents as the things of spirit are laid hold upon together, bringing new joy with each unfoldment of some great truth, with each fine new value laid hold upon more firmly, with each strong useful quality lived more surely.

1

HONESTY

TRUE HONESTY is of the spirit, reflecting fairness, justice, uprightness, sincerity, genuineness, honor in every act.

Honest action emanates from an honest thought. It is here that it has its roots. An honest thought admits of no hypocrisy, deceit or simulation. It partakes of no sham or pretense. It turns away from anything less than fair and just. It is marked with an integrity that unfailingly elicits respect. It is a thought sincere and genuine in its desire to know the right and to live it truly.

A thought that is truly honest is forever open and receptive to fresh revelation of what is right and true. It is pliable and flexible, unobstructed by prejudice or stubborn opinion and ready, even eager, for new light on what is fair and just. It is a searching thought, diligent and persistent in seeking the truth for the truth's sake, and never warping, perverting, distorting, or withholding it to suit either the purpose of expediency or selfish interest. An individual activated by such a thought strives to obey faithfully the principles he holds to be right without accepting even in thought any reservation or compromise that would mar the integrity of their expression.

It is an honest thought that restrains one from expressing judgment until facts can be known, from making decisions until every pertinent factor has been brought to light and considered without prejudice.

It is an honest thought that seeks always to accord others their rights with no attempt or wish to maneuver or manipulate them to one's own ends either through ruse, cunning artifice, or unfair stratagem. It is an honest thought that would avoid ever seeking to control another's thinking or take from him anything that is his, whether tangible possessions, credit that he has earned, creative ideas that are his, or the love, respect, and good name that belong to him. An honest thought holds inviolate the rights of others even as one's own.

This is honesty of a high order. It is achieved only by striving. It can be achieved only by first envisioning that this and nothing less is what honesty truly is.

But some may ask, "Is not honesty such as this stern, austere, cold, almost ruthless in its absoluteness?" Not when it is lighted with love as any spiritual quality must be, since all are intertwined. It is love that keeps honesty from being harsh in its justice, that makes it kindly and compassionate in its fairness, and unselfish in every act.

Can a child learn honesty such as this? Yes. With parents' help, honesty can unfold in a child's thought as a way of living that he accepts as right; a way of living that makes him known as a child of integrity; that brings respect to him because of that integrity; that lets him look fearlessly at all people because he knows that he is dealing truly with them; that gives him peace within because he knows that he is being true to himself.

There are many details about honesty for parents to help a child to think about and to help him to put into action. It takes honesty of thought to look squarely at one's reasons for having done something, to be wholly willing to look at them, to admit straightforwardly what those reasons are. This is honesty for which a child has daily need: the honesty to see clearly that he didn't really forget what Mother had said to do, he just didn't want to do it; the honesty to face the fact that he knew it was not quite fair to drive a sharp bargain in his marble exchange with a friend and that the real reason he did it was to get that coveted aggie—not, as he had first said, to give his friend the ones the friend wanted; the honesty to admit that it was well understood that the flowers should not have been picked without the neighbor's knowledge.

There are other motives for a child to recognize and be equally honest about. There is the genuine desire to be helpful that lies behind the offer to do the dusting; the wish to make another happy that prompts the giving of a treasured possession; the earnest desire to be dependable that is the real reason for faithful and cheerful performance of responsibilities. These too are motives for a child to be honest about.

Honesty with playmates is important for a child to understand: playing fair in a game, never cheating even a little bit to win; honesty in dividing evenly whatever is to be shared; honesty in saying "I was wrong" when differences arise and such was the case; honesty in admitting one's share in those differences and in genuinely trying to find a way to resolve them. There is the honesty to be learned that restrains one from ever taking anything that belongs to another without his knowledge or consent, an honesty that springs from such respect for another's rights that there is no desire to infringe upon them.

There are many things here to talk with a child

about. Often they are little things that he may not even be aware have to do with honesty until it is pointed out: things like taking a piece of fruit in a store without paying for it; taking things home that are school property and should be left there; keeping a friend's book when he knows it should be returned; making no effort to find the owner of a lost article because the child really wants to keep it.

A child can readily come to see that cheating in schoolwork is taking that which belongs to another just as much as taking any material possession; that taking credit for what another has done is taking what rightfully belongs to him; that cheating at a game is taking from him his right to win; that making a disturbance in the classroom is taking from the others their right to the teacher's time and attention; that keeping silent and letting blame that is one's own fall on another is taking from him a part of his good reputation; and that gossip and repeating or making slighting and belittling remarks are doing the same.

These may seem like little things in themselves; but no act is inconsequential that bears on the living of honesty, no thought is unimportant that helps a child to an understanding of what honesty truly is.

There is honesty concerning money to be thought about. This is a kind of honesty that a child comes to take as a matter of course when his parents set the example: when they buy no more than what they fully intend to pay for; when they correct an excess of change given them at the check-out counter; when they are fair and square about reporting all income on tax returns; when they would scorn to wangle vacation costs out of business expense accounts; when they never brag about making a profitable deal that was less than fair to another. With example such as this, a child can learn to be honest too in his money deal-ings. He can learn to give a fair amount of work for money received; to give a straightforward accounting for the use of his allowance if such accounting is asked; to buy only within the limits of what he can afford; to expect to repay in full anything he has borrowed.

As a child grows, he can learn that there is honesty to be considered in the opinions he expresses, in the convictions he sets forth, in the principles by which he professes to live. Only when honestly meant should they be spoken. Then, having been spoken, the only honest action is to strive to live them. This points to honesty of thought and action combined. The inner thought, the outward action: each must be truly fitted to the other, or else true honesty is lacking. The out-ward action without the inner thought, while it may have a practical usefulness, is but a sham; it is wholly devoid of sincerity, which is an essential component of true honesty.

24

Even the familiar adage, "Honesty is the best policy," takes honesty only to the point of being performed for selfish interest. It lacks the high purpose of rightful living for the pure sake of its rightness. Honesty lived because of fear of punishment is likewise devoid of high purpose and can never be rightly named as honesty. It is only the outward form put on as a garment for purposes of expediency.

Honesty is rightly named a spiritual quality only when it has its source in an honest thought; when action comes from that thought and is consistent with it. Such honesty is the epitome of integrity, an integrity that reaches into all of one's relationships with others and colors all of one's thought about himself.

These are big learnings for a child but children are equal to big learnings. These are steps in the unfolding of character, important steps. They are something for parents to start on with a very little child and to continue through all the growing years. The learning of them comes about when parents treat the child with the same honesty that they want him to learn to express, when they live honestly in his sight, when they talk with him about what honesty is, when they help him to see it as a thing of spirit and an expression of his own best self.

2

TRUTHFULNESS

W<small>HEN ONE SPEAKS</small> of teaching a child truthfulness, it is speaking the truth that first comes to mind. Truthfulness is the expression of a thought that sees the truth clearly and speaks it accurately and exactly. Truthfulness is a part of living truly. A thought from which the truth honestly is spoken is a true thought. Truthfulness is an essential element in high morality, a necessary part of any code of ethics because it is wholly good and real. In it there is no room for falsity, for evasion, for words that would deceive, for any intentional misrepresentation. There is no room for distortion of facts, for false coloring of those facts, for willful concealment or calculating dissimulation. The truth is ever pure, unadulterated, uncontaminated by anything unreal.

A thought that is true is a thought that is sincere and genuine. There is no place in it for duplicity, hypocrisy or bad faith in any form. A true thought is the very essence of realness, of principle, of honor. Out of such a thought only truthfulness could ever come. This is the kind of thought one would have a child learn to hold, a thought filled with the love of good of which truthfulness is a natural expression; a thought faithful in its fidelity to good; a thought loyal and steadfast in its adherence to what it sees to be the truth.

A true thought is inextricably interwoven with honesty. It is a reliable, dependable thought, a thought wholly worthy of trust. It is a fine, pure thought because it emanates from the good, from Spirit.

It is teaching a child the sure and only basis for truthfulness when one teaches him to love the right and good and to want to express it. Little children are readily receptive to the thought of good. They are eagerly willing to do the right. They are spontaneously zealous in expressing it when the understanding unfolds to them of what the right and good is, and when they see how to live it truly. It is for parents to give the help that brings this discernment and understanding in order that truthfulness in thought, word, and action shall become an established quality in the child's living.

It is discernment that enables the child to distinguish between fact and fancy and thus lets him see clearly the truth one would have him speak. It is lack of accuracy in this discernment, not intentional untruthfulness, that accounts for a little child's fanciful recountals told for fact. It is only as discernment becomes ever clearer that he can clearly and surely distinguish between what is in reality the fact and what in his fancy seems to be. It is help then in discernment between the two that is needed rather than bald admonitions to "tell me the truth."

It is not only clear discernment between fact and fancy that is needed to bring forth the truth. There is needed as well the remembering of details of occurrences sufficiently to speak the truth about them. Those details slip easily from memory; or because of preoccupation at the moment of their happening, never were clearly etched on thought. Then when the admonition comes to "tell me the truth," there is only the vague and clouded memory to draw upon, and the only true answer a child can give is, "I don't know." It is literally true that he does not know what the truth is that he is supposed to tell.

There is patience needed and deep understanding in great measure as parents seek to help a child to know where the truth lies and to tell it accurately. As one talks with him, he can come to see that it means telling things just as they are and not as he thought or wished they might have been; admitting just what he did or did not do instead of hiding or glossing over any part of it; stating another's part in whatever the situation may have been with equal accuracy.

There is the truthfulness to mention that precludes embellishing a tale with details which were no part of the actual happenings; or recounting events with oneself occupying the place of hero or heroine though such was far from being the fact; or telling of occurrences in such a way as to belittle or minimize the part that friends may have had in them while magnifying one's own.

A child can come to see that truthfulness plays a part in all of his relationships with others; that it has to do with his fairness, his loyalty, his friendliness in dealing with them; that upon it hinges much of their respect for him and of his own respect for himself, a respect justly earned when he has been wholly truthful and so to be rightfully enjoyed.

There is truthfulness of action which is a part of living truly and which one needs to help a child to think about: being true to what one understands to be right so that every act is in accord with the principles in which one believes; being true to what one inwardly knows to be right even though beset by plausible arguments to act otherwise; being true to one's own finer self and never stooping to actions that are unworthy.

Acting truly precludes the duplicity of saying one thing and doing another which is contradictory to it. It precludes the deceptiveness that either through silence, manner or gesture would intentionally mislead. It precludes any actions that would through pretense or artifice make one seem to be what one is not. It makes impossible actions that would give the appearance of honesty when back of them lies dishonesty of thought and intent. When acting truly there can never be the covering of wrong with the appearance of right.

All of this, a child can come to understand, is a part of living truly, a part of making his actions speak truthfully as surely as his word. This is consistency that is ever the mark of genuine truthfulness, consistency of thought, word and action in living the good as one sees it.

Truthfulness being an integral part of true living is of the spirit and from thence derives the moral courage necessary to its unwavering expression. This it is that enables a child to admit when he has done wrong even though there is dread of the punishment that may follow. This it is that makes it possible for him to sum-

31

mon the stamina to remain true to what he knows is right even in the face of ridicule and derision from playmates.

Truthfulness in word and deed always calls for courage: courage to speak the truth when it would be easier to keep silent; courage to say openly and truthfully, "I do not believe in doing thus and so" when it would be easier merely to profess dislike for whatever friends are enticing one to do; courage to state straightforwardly, "My parents do not want me to do thus and so" instead of pretending to indifference to the matter in question.

As parents talk with their children about truthfulness in all of their living they often query, "Must we always tell all the truth?" or "What if the truth is going to get someone else in trouble, wouldn't it be better to keep still?" or "What if we know the truth is going to hurt someone's feelings and we don't want to?" or "What about just a little tiny white lie that doesn't make any difference?"

The answers lie in the seeing of truthfulness as a spiritual quality intertwined with the wisdom and love that are themselves spiritual qualities, the wisdom that guides in knowing when to speak and when to withhold speech, the love that forever softens word and act with its warmth, kindness, gentleness. A child can learn that not all of the truth need always be spoken but all that is spoken must be true. He can learn to be slow in interpreting another's acts lest in that interpretation he wrongly assess the motive back of them. He can learn to look through outward actions that he may not like to the fineness that is the friend's true self and speak truly of that. He can learn that white lies so-called are deviations from the truth, and being deviations, they are not the truth; and that by deviation he has been less than truthful.

The truth need not be brutal. It is the way of speaking it, the time of speaking it, that makes it often seem less than kind. Truth spoken with wisdom and love can never harm. It can only bless. Whatever there may be of wrong it corrects. All of good, it magnifies.

As parents help a child to understand what truthfulness is in word and deed and to want to live it, they are helping him to the unfolding of character that makes him attractive to others, that brings respect to him, that gives him the inner peace and calm that true living ever brings.

3

COURAGE

TRUE COURAGE is a thing of the spirit. Like every other spiritual quality it is the outward expression of fine, true inner thought. It has its roots in an understanding of the right, a deep and true love for it, a staunch fidelity to it.

True courage is moral courage. It encompasses that physical bravery which goes beyond unthinking animal prowess because it is the showing forth of a spiritual value held high in thought as a guide to action. It is moral bravery which resolutely holds its ground for that which is accepted as right, with or without the accompaniment of physical valor.

The good, the right, the true, have ever been the bases for all real courage. Courage is a spiritual and moral quality which makes the problems of the day to be seen as opportunities for achievement. It is a quality with which one unwaveringly, intrepidly and with confidence holds to the right on which he has set his sights.

Is it, one asks, too much to expect of a child to bring courage such as this to his daily living? No, it is never too much to expect a child to take to himself the spiritual values which he can learn to express in spiritual and moral qualities daily lived. It is natural for him to do so. He takes things of the spirit into thought with simple acceptance and day by day with loving guidance the ways of expressing them can unfold to him.

Courage grows with use. Every day brings its opportunities to help a child to see where it is needed in his living and how he can put it into action. Resisting the temptation to be disobedient or less than truthful takes on a new importance when a child realizes that he has put courage into action if he turns away from that which would tempt him. He can come to see that the very fact of his reaching out for courage to do what he knows is right puts temptation to rout because he has put himself on the side of right and right always has power.

Children raise many questions as parents talk to them of courage, questions that are a searching for deeper understanding, questions that call for thoughtful answers if one would help that understanding to unfold. "What does my courage look like?" they ask. "Where do I get my courage, did you buy it for me?" "How do I know if I've got some courage?" "Where do I keep it?" "Has everybody got some?"

With parents' help even a very little child can come to understand that courage comes from good; that it is a Godlike quality; that it is an expression of good; that it is in one's thinking; that while one cannot see it one can feel it and can see what it makes one do; that all around one can see the things that other people do that show their courage.

A child can learn that it is courage that it takes to do what he knows is right when he feels frightened about doing it. Parents who tell their children Bible stories will tell of Moses with his courage in leading his people out of Egypt; of David, who protected his flocks of sheep fearlessly and faced the giant Goliath undauntedly; of Daniel, who showed no fear in the lion's den; and others, all of whom pointed to their trust in God as the source of their courage.

Courage has in it stamina, fortitude, resoluteness, firmness, the strength to stand, the endurance to hold to the course, the determination that remains steadfast in face of all that would divert or weaken, steady constancy, and clear-sightedness that keeps the value being upheld ever in sight.

"No, not any for me," said a sixteen-year-old when friends at a party produced some bottles of liquor, boasting of having laid their hands upon it though well knowing that it should never have been sold to them. "Afraid you'll get caught, uh?" jibed one. "Better run out," jeered another, "before anything happens to Mama's boy." "No," said the boy, "it's not that. I don't believe in drinking and I'm not doing it." With that the jeers and jibes flew thick and fast. He stood his ground. "Call me a poor sport if you want to," he said, "but I am not drinking." And he didn't. That took courage.

It took courage for ten-year-old Jerry to get himself to school one lovely spring morning when fishing looked much more enticing than school. Two bigger boys were daring him to join them but he didn't go. That night when he told Mother about it he said, "I had to run fast so I wouldn't change my mind and do it." Mother gave the commendation deserved in good measure. She did not leave it there, though. "Have you thought just why you didn't go?" she asked. "No," he said, "I just knew I ought not to because I was supposed to go to school but I sure did want to." "Did you know," she asked, "that you were using the courage we have talked about when you stuck to it that you wouldn't do what you knew was wrong?" "Was it because I didn't have much of it that I had to run or I might do it?" he asked. "No," said Mother, "I'd say that it took a good deal of courage to start yourself running so that you would be sure not to do it." It is just such talks as this that help a child to think clearly about courage to live according to his highest sense of right.

It took courage for thirteen-year-old Dema to say that she was sorry for the angry words she had spoken to her friend Nancy. It meant admitting to herself that she too had been wrong. It meant setting her pride aside before she could speak the words that acknowledged it. It meant silencing the self-justification which came pouring forth as she told Mother how Nancy had been so wrong and how "anyone with any sense would have been just as mad at her as I was." It meant turning away from the thought of self to the thought of what was fair and honest. It always takes courage to move self out of the light so that the spiritual value one holds is right may be more clearly seen and more truly expressed.

One often hears it said, "He has the courage of his convictions." Seventeen-year-old Mart had learned to have that courage and to use it. He had been on the student council for a year. He felt that decisions were being made too hastily and pushed through by a few and that they were not always made with the best interests of all students in mind. He had spoken of it often. Then as he neared the end of his term of service he took a vigorous stand about it. It was not a belligerent stand but a forthright, vocal, unequivocal one. He talked with the principal and with his adviser about it. With their knowledge and approval he discussed it with leaders of the various organized groups and with other representative students. He stood with the courage of his convictions. To do such as this one must have convictions in the first place; know what they are; why one believes in them; then have the stamina to stand for them.

Six-year-old Janet had the beginnings of some convictions and she stood by one of them valiantly. It meant a physical tussle with two boys to rescue a kitten that they were teasing and tormenting. She used her fists. She kicked and scratched. She bit. She screamed for Mother, but before Mother got there the boys had taken to their heels and she had the kitten.

It was a blind sort of courage that rescued that kitten but it was dauntless and it was born of conviction. It was a tiny little conviction but already strong enough to bring forth the courage to defend it, courage that transcended any thought of personal danger.

As a child grows convictions deepen, and as they become increasingly clarified the courage to hold to them strengthens and moves from a blind, unthinking defense to a reasoned, considered one. Deep convictions bring courage with them, for strong convictions cannot lie dormant. They push for expression and only through courage can they find that expression.

It is thus that creative forward-reaching and useful ideas come to fruition in action. Without the accompaniment of courage they remain only ideas unexpressed and lost in the mediocrity above which with courage they might rise. Somewhere, sometime, in the thought of someone, came the idea, for example, to turn destructive high school and college hazing into useful social service. Because courage accompanied the idea many have been helped; not only those for whom the thoughtful, useful deeds have been done, but the doers as well. One can only imagine the courage needed in this and in many other instances to stem the tide of destructive actions and to turn an energy worse than wasted into useful direction.

All around a child in any neighborhood, in any community, there lie instances to be seen of those who have had the courage to hold to an idea that has reached beyond the thinking around them. It can be an inspiration to a child to have those instances brought into his awareness. History is full of them. Every new movement, every invention, every reform, every great humanitarian service, has been an idea revealed to someone who was able to grasp it and who had courage to bring it into action. A child can come to see that it takes courage not only for the one with the idea to hold to it, but for others to come to its support despite the resistance that new ideas are sure to bring.

A child has need for courage to meet the disappointments along the way he travels in his daily living. It takes courage to meet disappointments with thinking and constructive action instead of with weeping: a courage that will have none of self-pity; that will accept no suggestion of defeat; that turns the situation to some useful purpose. There is persistence in this kind of courage, persistence in looking for the good in every experience, persistence in taking that and only that into one's thought.

It takes courage of a high order to persistently set aside the suggestions that argue for discouragement, that whisper that it is no use to try; that the situation is impossible; that one is not equal to it. It takes courage to silence the suggestions that it is foolish to put forth full effort when one could easily get by with less; that by playing on another's good nature or appealing through flattery he could be cajoled into doing the work that is rightfully one's own. It takes courage to set aside the thought that others are standing in the way of what one might accomplish; that their envy, hatred, jealousy, or even their success would so hamper one's efforts as to make them useless. A child can learn to see that these are only arguments which bring nothing useful into his living and that when he faces them with courage, they disappear. Each experience in which he uses courage adds to the courage he has in his thought ready for further use.

Courage is a dynamic, vital, active quality. It is never apathetic, passive, evasive, or indecisive. Even when there has to be the courage to wait, to be patient, to ponder, to defer decision, it is still a dynamic quality. A waiting with courage is watchful, alert waiting. Patience with courage is active, thoughtful, understanding patience, never a resigned martyr-like defeatist patience. Pondering, considering, deferring of decision when deferring seems wise, necessitates the use of a more active, conscious, intelligent courage than the brash, hasty, impulsive courage that would lead one into plunging thoughtlessly ahead.

True courage intertwines with every other spiritual quality. It is an inherent part of them. It is courage that enables one to be gentle in place of any impulse to be harsh; to be forgiving instead of resentful or revengeful; to be humble instead of arrogant; to meet aggression with the will to peace though fighting might be easier; to fight when need be in defense of a principle which can be upheld in no other way; to take all of living despite its difficulties with that joy which is in itself a spiritual quality.

This is courage of great strength. It is courage tha

strengthens moral fiber, courage that makes one dare to be loving, kind, tender, compassionate, even while being firm, resolute and dauntless in a holding to the right as one sees it. It is a courage that leads one on in a fearless search for ever deeper insight into the right and a willingness to follow one's highest sense of it as it is revealed in thought.

Are children equal to this? one may ask. Are these not concepts deep in their implications and difficult in their performance? Yes, they are both, but children are capable of depth of thought, and difficulties challenge them. Courage comes to them easily and naturally just as do other spiritual qualities, for their thought is pure; their faith is simple and steadfast; their acceptance of good is unquestioning and willing; their impulse to action is forthright and fearless until fears come from outside their own thought.

This courage which a child reflects so naturally can easily become a part of his everyday way of living when parents give the thoughtful, understanding guidance that helps him to learn how to use it with consideration for others; with adherence to the principles taught to him as right; with fidelity to those principles he himself comes to see are right as he grows.

Courage begets courage. A child who lives in the midst of courageous living has before him the example which speaks to him of courage as directly as any words spoken to him about it. Together the example and the words spoken make up the guidance that helps him to have the courage to live with courage.

4

RESPONSIBILITY

Responsibility is an active, dynamic quality. It is reaction to a situation with a sense of individual obligation. True responsibility stems from spiritual and moral values held in thought as right and true, and the feeling of necessity to express them in action. True responsibility is intertwined with every other spiritual and moral quality, for it is only through a sense of obligation for expressing them that they can come into action.

Responsibility denotes moral integrity, dependability, trustworthiness. There is no room in it for leaving one's work for another to do or for being careless in the doing of it. There is no room in it for making idle statements without fact to support them; or for behaving in ways that are unprincipled; or for refusing to be answerable for whatever one may have said or done; or for being in any way unreliable in word or action.

Responsibility has in it steadfastness, faithfulness, a continuance in any obligation which one has agreed to carry. It partakes of uprightness, honor, honesty, truthfulness.

True responsibility holds one ever to his highest sense of right with the feeling of obligation to express that rightness in daily living. It is a holding true to the principles in which one believes. It is a striving ever to bring principles and action into coincidence. It is a quality that touches every phase of living, every phase of relationships with others.

Responsibility such as this encompasses all lesser responsibilities, all those everyday details of living that one would have a child take to himself. It gives meaning to them. It is this wide, broad, true thought of responsibility that parents do well to set their sights on as they attempt to teach the lesser details. It is this higher sense of responsibility one would have a child himself envision even as he learns to carry through the faithful performance of details that fall to him to do. It is this that puts the lesser details into their proper setting.

Responsibility comes naturally and easily to little children. They want to be responsible. They like to be.

48

They derive immense satisfaction from being allowed to be. Often one sees the little child's eagerness to do things for himself as only budding independence, missing entirely the beginnings of responsibility equally as important as the independence. The two ever go hand in hand, and as growing goes on there comes the need for learning that one must ever be responsible for using independence wisely and well. This it is that helps the child when the teen years have come to hold in check that urge for independence that, without the responsibility, lures into pathways better unexplored.

As a child grows he finds things, one after another, which he can do for himself and eagerly claims the right to do them. The responsibilities may in themselves be small—the taking off of clothes, the washing of hands, the feeding himself instead of being fed—but the willingness is big. This is very precious to keep. Willingness is ever a basic ingredient of responsibility that is accepted or assumed cheerfully.

Even though in those beginnings there is little of the sense of obligation that is the mark of true responsibility, yet it is here that it has its roots. Nor need there be delay in even the little child's learning that there is obligation incumbent upon him, the obligation to do willingly what parents say; the obligation to carry through with tasks they assign; the obligation as he grows to follow rules and regulations even though parents are not at hand to enforce them; the obligation to do his work at school faithfully and well.

Very early there begins to appear that insight and perceptiveness essential to the voluntary assuming of responsibility, the insight that opens one's eyes to what needs to be done, the perceptiveness that brings the mental image of the portion one himself might do. These, too, are beginnings to be cherished.

Eleven-year-old Elaine and her brother Henry, thirteen, had insight, and the perceptiveness as well as the willingness, to assume a responsibility which they had envisioned themselves as taking. Their mother had been trying to plan a way that she might enroll for a university extension course being given in the community. The meeting hours, four to six-thirty, made it seem impossible, since the half-hour drive following class meant a much-too-late dinner. Elaine and Henry, though, had a plan. They would get the dinner that one evening of the week. They were confident of their ability to do it. They were eager to prove that they could. They were undaunted at the thought of its being an undertaking of fifteen weeks' duration. They would stick to it, they said. Furthermore, they would not "fuss and quarrel" while they did it. They kept their word. They carried the responsibility without wavering throughout the entire time.

That took self-discipline. Being responsible by its

very nature calls for self-discipline; for holding oneself to the task regardless of diversions that beckon; for continuing on to the completion of the undertaking despite any waning interest and enthusiasm; for conscientious performance of whatever is to be done albeit there may be little liking for it. A responsible thought is a self-disciplined thought always. It holds itself responsible. It does not have to be held. This is true, independent responsibility. A child can learn it when parents help him to do so.

This is learning which goes beyond the mere doing of tasks because the parent's watchful eye is upon him. It is doing the task because it should be done and because it is one's individual obligation to do it. This is a learning upon which to set one's sights even while providing the insistence that holds a child to what he is supposed to do until such time as he can hold himself to it. It is a learning which comes best when the child sees the task in its relation to the living of which it is a part. This gives the reason for the doing, whether it be to one's liking or not.

Here lies the answer to objections to the making of beds, the washing of dishes, the care of garbage, the dusting of the house, the keeping of one's room tidy. These tasks that understandably get irksome in their daily recurrence can come to look very different when seen as necessary to making home livable, and just as

51

all rightfully share in the enjoyment of a livable home, so all rightfully must share in making it so. The task to be done thus becomes a means to an end, not an end in itself. The taking of responsibility is the matter of importance. The doing of the task well becomes the measure of the way the responsibility is performed. The spirit with which it is done bespeaks the underlying feeling which alone can bring satisfaction out of the most humdrum work.

A child can, with help, learn that a willing, loving spirit is just as much a part of his responsibility as doing well the actual task which he performs. When one helps him to see that he is responsible for his inner feelings and thoughts and that he can say what they shall be, one has gone directly to the root of all action. When a child learns to control his thoughts and make them right, he is learning the one sure way to control his actions and make them right. This is responsibility of a high order.

"What kind of thoughts have you been thinking tonight?" asked a mother at bedtime of an eight-year-old who had been sulking throughout the evening.

"They're mad ones," said the child, "but I can't help it. Everybody made me mad today." Then she launched into a tale of grievances.

"I'd be interested to know," said the mother, "how

anyone can make you think mad thoughts unless you want to."

Then they talked again as they had often done before about how each person is responsible for his own thinking and how no one can make you think mad thoughts if you refuse to think them and put others in their place. Just so a child can learn that no one can make him act in a way that he does not wish to act, that he alone is responsible for his behavior, responsible for being obedient—for keeping his word, for being truthful and honest, for doing what he knows to be right.

Responsibility is a quality that reaches into every part of a child's living—his home living, his school living, his church living, his community living. The sense of responsibility which he brings to that living determines in a large measure both what he puts into it and what he gets out of it. It reaches into every aspect of his relationships with playmates. It has to do with the part he takes in all of their work and play together. It determines in great measure their feelings about him, for unless there is responsibility for being considerate, thoughtful, kind, those relationships lack the warmth and richness that make them lasting, useful, rewarding. It has to do with his feelings about himself, for the conscious feeling of being responsible brings its own self-respect, its own assurance, the satisfying awareness of having done one's part, of having adhered faithfully to what one knows to be right and fine. Responsibility has to do with a child's achievement and accomplishments, with his diligence in pursuing whatever the work at hand may be, with the honest effort he puts into it, with the use to the fullest of the talents brought to it.

Teaching a child to act with true responsibility entails teaching him to feel responsible; to see himself as being responsible; to be willing and glad to be responsible; to accept the fact that he should be responsible —and then to be so. As with all other qualities, it is the thought and feeling which give rise to the action and must never be neglected if living is to have the mark of genuineness and sincerity.

A sense of responsibility for bringing into action his highest understanding of good can grow as a child grows, and as parents help him to see more and more deeply into the things of Spirit and to feel not only the obligation but the privilege of expressing them. It is responsibility that holds one always to his highest sense of right. It is a quality whose deeper meanings unfold as experience broadens, insight becomes clearer, and sensitivity to need more sure. As that comes about, thought reaches farther and farther beyond itself with a wider and deeper concern for others and for their well-being. There comes then that sense of individual responsibility that leads into participation in community movements that are for the good of all, into wider world affairs, into general responsibility for doing whatever one can that good may be expressed.

As parents strive to guide a child in the learning of responsibility their own willingness to *let* responsibility be taken in daily affairs encourages its being so taken whether the child be two, ten, or in the teens. Reasonableness in number and kind of tasks assigned tends to insure the acceptance of responsibility for them with good grace. Thoughtfulness in being watchful that those tasks become neither unduly burdensome nor monotonous brings appreciation that increases the willingness to accept other tasks as they are given. Consideration in helping the child to see how to do the things that are asked of him gives him the assurance and confidence that enable him to perform them in acceptable ways. Commendation when they have been well and faithfully done brings satisfaction that begets willingness.

Offering a choice of tasks to be undertaken brings a welcome sense of independence and self-direction that increases the sense of responsibility. Leaving the responsibility for doing the tasks with a minimum of supervision bespeaks a trust that brings self-respect, satisfaction in being worthy of trust, and an added feeling of obligation and desire to be thus worthy.

Helping the child to see the responsibilities that are rightfully his opens the way for him to voluntarily assume their doing. It is leading him into feeling responsible for being responsible. Talking with him about the usefulness of his responsible acts brings the understanding that this is the way of taking his part in bringing good to others as well as to himself, the way of taking his place among them as a useful, contributing person worthy of their respect.

With guidance such as this, a child can come to see responsibility not as a burden, arbitrarily imposed upon him, but as the joyous privilege of acting in that free, independent, dependable, reliable manner which makes others respect him and makes him respect himself.

As parents seek to teach their children true responsibility there is sure to unfold to them, too, its deeper meanings, and with that unfolding the feeling of solemn obligation and priceless privilege to teach it truly and worthily. No greater service can be done a child than to help him learn to feel a free, happy, joyous responsibility for knowing and doing the right. Never can responsibility that is the expression of the true spiritual quality be burdensome, interwoven as it is with the other qualities of Spirit, and because of that, glowing always with the joy and love that keep it gladsome.

5

GENEROSITY

Generosity which is sincere and honest, and there can rightly be no other, has its source in a generous thought. A generous thought is a giving thought. It is a thought that reaches out to another or others with good. It is always an outgoing, never a withdrawing or withholding, thought. It is gladsome and joyous because it comes out of a sense of good and carries that sense with it. It is free, spontaneous, hearty, full of good feeling.

The generosity which is the expression of such a thought brings enrichment and blessing to the child who learns to make it a part of his living, and to all those whom his living touches. They in turn are blessed.

There is much of guidance needed to help a child in bringing the quality of generosity to its fullest and finest expression, for it relates directly not only to consideration and thoughtfulness for others but to honesty, sincerity and humility as well.

Eight-year-old Janice gave and gave to friends and classmates. She gave pencils, pennies, jackstones, jumping rope, and would have given her favorite doll had Mother not called a halt. This was giving but it was not generosity. It was giving that was without either honesty or sincerity. It was giving in the hope of finding favor with the other children, giving for a selfish purpose, giving for personal gain.

Giving which is truly generous is unselfed giving without purpose of personal advantage, gain or glory as its motivating factor. It is giving with a thought that is outgoing, never inturning nor self-seeking.

"I gave Allen my red aggie today," said an eight-year-old marble player to his mother. "How did you happen to do that?" she asked. "Oh," said the child, "he wanted it so I gave it to him." "That was generous," she said, "and I know he must have appreciated it." But she soon discovered it was not generous. Ten marbles had been exacted in return for the one.

Then that mother talked with the child about what giving really is and about what being generous is. "You didn't really give him anything," she told him. "You traded with him. If it was an honest trade and you both were satisfied, that was all right, but it was not giving." There was learning for that child in that experience because the mother was thoughtful about what giving truly is and meant that he too should come to understand it. It takes keen discernment to see what one's motive for giving is, and sincere, honest thought to be willing to turn the light of discernment on it that one may see it truly.

Genuine generosity is more than sharing when told to share. "Let him play with some of your toys," a mother says to the two-year-old who is trying to gather all of his playthings within the circle of his arms, safe from the one who is reaching for them. "Here, give him these," she insists, taking some from him and handing them to the other child. "You mustn't keep everything yourself, you must learn to be more generous."

The sharing which is done when another says it must be is obedience and compliance. It is not generosity. It may be a step in learning to be generous but it is not in itself generosity, because it does not spring from an inner thought that wants to give.

"Which toy could you let him play with?" says another mother to another two-year-old. "He wants to play, too. Would you give him one of your toys to play with?"

Out of his feeling of having his toys she is asking him to be willing to give of his toys. There must always be the feeling of having before there can ever be the feeling of giving, otherwise there is nothing of which to give whether it be material things or love, goodwill, helpfulness. Giving is reaching forth with what one has. Generous giving is reaching forth abundantly, unstintedly, liberally, bountifully, heartily.

Four-year-old Ena had been busy with paper and colored pencils all the while that Mother and Grandmother, who had come for the day, were sewing and talking. All at once she went to Grandmother with a drawing in hand. "It's for you," she said. "It's my most beautifulest one I made, and see what it says down there. It says I love you." This was giving that was done freely, spontaneously, joyously. Both the "I love you" and the manner of giving told of the genuinely loving thought out of which the gift had come.

It was that which made it rich far beyond its material appearance. It is always the loving thought which gives value to a gift. It is the abundance of the love that makes the giving generous. This a child can learn.

The way to the learning is to help the child to think abundantly, to help him to fill his thought with kindness, friendliness, goodwill. Then it becomes natural to give, because thought is overflowing with something fine to give and the giving out of its fullness cannot be withheld.

As a child learns to think generously it comes easy for him to express generosity in the way he takes responsibility, in the way he speaks appreciation, in the way he offers encouragement to another, in the way he gives credit where credit is due, in the way he comes forth with helpful acts whenever he sees that help is needed, in the way he gives of effort to whatever he has to do.

Giving generously in the taking of responsibility is giving beyond that which is asked. It is in assuming it when it has not been asked, and putting effort forth liberally, that what is done may be one's best. This kind of giving lifts the taking of responsibility above a duty to be performed to a loving service to be given.

Giving generously makes the speaking both of appreciation and encouragement a free, spontaneous, genuine thing, an offering of words that come straight from the heart with no premeditation or calculation as to whether gain for oneself will come from the saying of them or not. The words of encouragement come forth from a thought that would help—those of appreciation from a grateful thought.

The generous giving of credit where credit is due has in it fairness and justice in such ample measure that, in combination with the kindliness and friendliness which are inherent in both, there could never be any withholding. These are thoughts that move aside the thoughts of self that would push one on to the grasping of credit as one's own. So it is with the generosity of feeling that enables one to graciously and willingly accord to another his chance and his right to a place of prominence and prestige. This is generosity indeed, for selfish interest would ever tempt to the ruthless gathering to oneself all of the honor, glory, recognition, prestige, acclaim, without regard to others. Giving generously of willingness that they should have their opportunity is genuine unselfish generosity. Rejoicing generously when they have honestly achieved it is outward evidence of thought filled full with goodwill.

A generous thought is ever a helpful thought, a thought that reaches out to others with the sincere wish to be of service. It is this that the little child is doing with his first offers of "help" with whatever it is that the grown-up is busy about. It is what eight- and ten-year-old Ted and Terry were doing when they brought Daddy all of their piggy-bank savings to give aid in a family emergency. It was what fifteen-year-old Nancy was doing when she gave her summer to volunteer work in a social agency.

As a child grows there can come that wider understanding of where help is needed, and that deeper insight into how to give it, that lead directly into that generosity in giving which finds expression in responsible community service.

Generosity in effort put forth is one of the marks of a truly generous thought. There could be no work left half-done or poorly done with such a thought, nor could there be any begrudging of the time needed for doing it well or any stinting on the time given to accomplish it.

A generous thought becomes more generous the more the giving to the point of being generous in forgiveness for wrongs one believes to have been done; generous in not demanding redress for those wrongs; generous with seeing another's good and not his faults; generous always with well-speaking about him. This is being generous with love.

Love is always intertwined with true generosity. So, likewise, is the wisdom that guides one in being generous wisely; that holds in check any unthinking impulse that, while springing from a loving thought, would take from another his right also to be generous.

"Do you realize," said a mother to her sixteen-year-old daughter, "that you are being very selfish about being generous?" Then she pointed out to the girl that in taking to herself responsibilities rightfully the privilege of others to carry she was giving, yes, but not wisely or thoughtfully, because she was depriving them of their own opportunity to give. It was a big thought which that mother offered to that girl.

Generosity must ever be tempered with wisdom, with good judgment, with sensitivity to equal rights of others, else it becomes selfish in the name of being generous. Generosity is never generous when it is selfish, nor is it then true generosity. It is only the outward form without the inner thought.

Generosity is a fruit of the spirit, a spiritual quality, a spiritual grace, a quality of principle. With parental guidance a child can learn to think the generous, loving thoughts out of which generosity comes. When he is helped to keep his mind open and receptive to good, those thoughts unfold naturally and easily. As parents help him to see the ways of bringing them into expression he can come to know the joy that the living of any spiritual quality brings with it. As they themselves live generously in his sight day by day, he catches the feeling of generous living. As they give generously to him of affection, time, appreciation, listening, commendation, trust, the feeling of generous living is woven into his living. Through the closeness of the family ties, it becomes a part of him and a way of life that he accepts as right and good.

6

PATIENCE

PATIENCE as a spiritual quality is vastly different from the long-suffering endurance which it is often taken to be, or tight-lipped resignation, or martyr-like acceptance of something not wholly liked. These are the negative, passive aspects of patience. They stem from a feeling of deprivation or of being visited with some calamity hard to bear or from a sense of the thwarting of some great desire. One might rightly question whether submission to such feelings can be properly named patience, since it differs so fundamentally from what patience truly is.

There is nothing passive or negative about true patience. It is dynamic, active, vigorous. It is a positive, forceful quality. It has none of weakness in it. It is a quality of strength and it brings strength of character to the one who learns to show it in his living. It is a quality that parents do well to help a child begin early to learn.

Even a little child has need for patience: patience when toys break; when pieces of puzzles will not fit together; when zippers will not zip; when fingers fumble and buttons will not button; when Mother says, "Come" just when he wants to play; when tricycle wheels catch on the post he is trying to ride around; when hands cannot quite manage the scissors with which he is trying to cut; when a playmate will not play as he wants him to; when parents say "No" to what he wants to do or to have. For a little child, a big child, a teen-ager, every day brings its need for patience in waiting for what he wants until it is right for him to have it; patience for taking with good grace situations not to his liking; patience in working out the difficulties that come his way; patience in sticking to what he has undertaken; patience with friends who do not see eye to eye with him; patience with himself when accomplishments he desires are slow of achievement; patience when disappointments come; patience in waiting for wisdom to know the thing that is best to do; patience when friends seem to be less than fair and loyal.

The patience for which a little child has need is exactly the same patience he will need during all the years. The situations in which he needs it will vary with his growing but the quality of patience needed to meet them is forever the same.

Like every spiritual quality, patience has intertwined with it other spiritual and moral qualities, each useful in itself but each strengthened because of its union with the patience that aids in its expression. A child can come to see this, and the seeing will bring more meaning and understanding to the admonition he hears so often: "Be patient, dear, be patient."

Sometimes patience looks unattractive to a child because there is so much of waiting in it. In the words of a five-year-old, "I would just as soon be patient if I didn't always have to wait, but I don't like to wait."

The child can learn that patient waiting is not inactive, passive, desultory waiting. "Wait until I finish the dishes," says Mother to her three-year-old, "and I'll read you the story." Then she adds, "If you will put the silver away, I'll get through sooner and we can read sooner because you will be helping me." The three-year-old does help. She waits; but it is active waiting, waiting that has in it the service which so often accompanies patient waiting. No fretting, no fussing, but instead a busy activity as the waiting goes on. One does well, however, not to prolong the waiting beyond the promised time lest in the stretching of time patience becomes taut.

"We'll have to wait," says a father to the nine-year-old who wants a new bicycle. "We'll have to wait until we get the money to buy it, and whatever you can earn or save out of your allowance, I'll match it and then you can have the bicycle." The waiting for that bicycle is active, waiting with useful, constructive activity directed toward a definite purpose.

Not all of the waiting that patience makes necessary is as tangibly active as this. The waiting of twelve-year-old Sandra was of another kind. "It is going to mean waiting until we can decide what it is best to do, but we'll think about it," her parents said. She had begun in midwinter to ask to go to camp the following summer. The necessary waiting for the decision was active, with thinking over plans for all of the family; with watching how developments in Father's business affected what would be financially possible; with consideration of the camps that would be desirable from the standpoints of distance, cost, and program. Here was waiting that brought thought of others and their needs, a weighing of values as a guide to decision, the use of good judgment in coming to that decision.

"You're not old enough yet," meant another kind of waiting for thirteen-year-old Ethel. She wanted to begin dating. "You can have the boys and girls here and you can go out with the crowd, but you will have to wait until you are older before you date," her parents said. That seemed like slow waiting, but the parents saw to it that it was very active waiting. Learning that all waiting can be usefully active is just as valuable as learning of the patience of which it is a part.

The true patience which is a spiritual quality brings with it no feeling of being perturbed, discontented, disgruntled, or resentful even when it means waiting. True patience has its roots in thought that sets aside self-will that would demand immediate action even though delay seems wise or necessary; or self-right-eousness that would claim to know exactly what should be done with no question as to its wisdom; or self-interest out of willingness to consider others.

Such a thought is a hopeful, joyous, buoyant thought because it is not weighted down with thought of self, which is always both obstructive and destructive. Patient waiting that comes out of this thought could never have in it anything of discouragement, despair, or frustration.

In teaching a child to learn to wait, one would never want to lose that sense of immediacy so characteristic of a childlike thought: that sense of living in the *now* with neither a backward nor a forward look but only the urgency, interest and joy of the present. That characteristic has great value. Kept through the years, it brings one to the living of each day as it comes without regret of the past or dread of the future. With it, however, can come the ability to wait actively and happily. This ability detracts nothing from joyous, useful living of the present. It rather enhances it because of preventing the feverish, petulant, anxious haste of impatience from ever becoming any part of it.

This is patience that has in it steadfastness, perseverance, faith in what one is doing and in one's ability to do it. This is the patience that holds one steadily, undauntedly, unflinchingly to the accomplishment of the task to which one has set himself, no matter whether he is a four-year-old trying to put together the big packing crates for a playhouse or the fifteen-year-old repairing the jalopy engine he has taken apart. It is the same patience that keeps each one at it instead of giving up with a defeatist "What's the use?" or an exasperated "I can't do it, someone has got to help me"; or wandering off in discouragement. It is patience with perseverance in it that keeps a nine-year-old trying and trying again, without tears or fussing, to weave the potholder that won't seem to come out straight, and that makes the sixteen-year-old write and rewrite the English theme until it sounds the way she wants it to sound.

"But," one asks, "may not this be dogged stubbornness rather than patience, a stubbornness that will not allow one to let go?" The spirit of the doing points the difference. There is nothing of hope or buoyancy in stubbornness; in patience, there is.

It can be a real inspiration to a child to know that the patience that carries him on in his efforts is of the same quality as that which has led people of all time to great discoveries and inventions and services to mankind. He can come to see that it was through true patience that the art of printing came into being; that the electric lights and the telephone we take for granted became realities; that many different plants have been propagated; that the airplane was perfected; that humanitarian services of many kinds have brought benefit to thousands.

One could go on and on with specific illustrations pointing to the great men and women of history who have exercised patience in carrying out ideas they believed in. One is wise to open the eyes of a child early to this broader view of the quality one would have him learn. It gives a new meaning to patience when he realizes that back of a thing such as the telephone stood someone with the patience to work perhaps for years on an idea in which he had faith, that there was a fidelity to purpose that held him unwaveringly. By patient effort one achieves. It is useful for a child to understand that with patience he, too, can achieve.

Patience with people is something for a child to

73

think about. This is patience that comes out of thoughts of kindliness, friendliness, consideration, love, loyalty. These thoughts find their natural expression in a forbearance with friends that not only silences any words of condemnation but never lets them be taken into thought. They are thoughts that make forgiveness easy when wrong has been done, thoughts that lead one to look past the wrong to all the good one knows about the friend. When disagreements rear their heads, or one is tempted to feel that someone has been irritating, annoying, unfair, or disloyal, these are thoughts that bring forth love, compassion, tenderness, instead of vexation, censure and blame.

"Well," said a mother to her eight-year-old, "you know we all make mistakes sometimes. Couldn't you think about what she did as just a mistake, and go on loving her anyway?"

"No," said the child, "she broke my doll carriage on purpose and I don't want to love her and I'm not going to."

The mother said, "Is that the way you want me to feel when you make a mistake? You seem to like it when I am patient about your mistakes. Couldn't you be patient about hers?"

That was a new idea but the child had an answer. "No," she said, "you're a grown-up and you're my mother and I'm not her mother and I don't have to be patient."

Then they talked about how other people besides mothers have to be patient, and how being patient with friends is part of being a friend oneself. They spoke of how forgiving and going on loving is part of being patient with people and how everyone is doing the best he can and it helps when we love instead of condemning.

Yes, these are big ideas. The sooner, though, that a child is helped to learn to think them, the sooner he will learn to live the qualities that express them. The more useful and happy living will then be for him and for everyone around him.

Patience with others is often easier for a child to learn than patience with himself. Patience with oneself does not mean complacency or self-righteous self-satisfaction. Far from it. Patience with oneself means striving and being willing to strive to live those values one holds to be right without indulging in self-condemnation, self-deprecation, discouragement, or despair when mistakes are made, but seeing mistakes instead as stepping-stones to learning. Such patience has in it the humility that brings willingness to learn; confidence in the ability to do it; joy in the opportunity. All bring strength to the patience which makes learning possible, and which never gives way to the obstruction of impatience.

A patient thought is a calm, quiet, composed thought. It has none of the strain, struggle, restlessness and stir that come with impatience, which by its very nature speaks of lack of peace, poise and equanimity. Impatience is in itself a form of anger, the way of irritability, tantrums, impulsive destructive action, petulance, explosive criticism. Patience is a form of love that has no willfulness in it, no arrogance, no peevish haste, but rather the willingness to let whatever it is best to do or say unfold in its own time and way. An active, alert patience signifies the confidence that the best will so unfold. It removes the sense of hurry, push, rush.

Patience relates always to all of the other spiritual and moral values one holds as right. It is these that point the way to what one shall be patient about. In turn, it is the patient striving to live these other values which brings them to human sight. It is wisdom, itself a spiritual quality, that reveals to the one who waits that now is the time to act or speak, or that the further withholding of action and speech is the highest right at the moment. Thus wisdom must always go hand in hand with patience so that action and speech will be neither too hasty nor too long delayed.

With its roots in spiritual thought, and its expression

guided by one's spiritual and moral values, patience that is alert, active, wise, kind and loving bespeaks trust and faith in good. Otherwise one would never be willing to wait, to endure, to persevere in effort, to steadfastly see the good in others, to defer decisions for greater light, to hold to kindly thought in place of vexations, to meet uncertainties without being distraught, to face difficulties with equanimity, to take disappointments without discontent and seemingly adverse circumstances with neither resentment nor self-pity.

Patience so defined has in it continuous recognition of good as being ever present; abiding confidence in the unfailing power of good; steadfast acknowledgment of good; unwavering expectation of good's continuous evidence. Patience has hope, faith, trust in it. Otherwise there would be little incentive to its exercise. Patience is a grace of the spirit, a grace in which a child can grow, a grace which unfailingly attracts with its serene good nature, its understanding, its kindliness and goodwill.

If one would have a child learn patience such as this, there must be patience in teaching it, the same patience one would have him learn: patience full of trust and confidence in him; patience full of consistency in what is asked of him; patience that has the fortitude to hold to the line one feels is right for him to follow; patience that never falters in its expectation of good from him; patience that has in it all the constancy of love that enfolds him in its warmth as his learning goes on; patience that comes from an abiding faith in the child's willingness to do right. Such patience brings hope, light, joy and gladness into all of the child's bringing up. It speaks clearly to him of what true patience is.

7

HUMILITY

IN THINKING of the spiritual and moral qualities that one wishes to teach a child, humility often goes unmentioned. Yet it is a quality essential in the building of truly harmonious relationships with others. It is a quality fundamentally basic to willing learning. It is a quality that attracts because it is kindly, generous, unselfish, free from swaggering arrogance, ostentatious self-importance, or the egotism that would demand to be forever the focus of attention.

Often it is assumed that it is a quality foreign to a little child's nature and so to be left for later teaching. Not so. This only mistakes the true nature of the child. No one is more teachable than a little child or more willing to learn. Humility is an inherent element in both. Here, then, one finds the quality a natural part of the child's individuality ready for unfolding, needing only the guidance that will bring it to fine fruition. It is guidance which should never be withheld or delayed.

Often it is assumed further that a little child has small need for humility. This too is a false assumption. There is daily need for it. One asks obedience of a child and humility is an essential element in willing and ready obedience. One asks the child to admit when he has been in the wrong. It takes humility to do so. Daily he has to be willing to accept ideas that playmates have for their play together, ideas that may not agree with his own. It takes humility to accede to them. Brothers and sisters tease. It is only with humility that one can take it with good grace.

No, from little childhood on, humility is an essential quality of living if that living is to be useful and harmonious. This is the time when learning how to live it should begin. As a child grows and the urge for independence and self-direction strengthens, it is humility and only humility that can bring the willingness to listen to parents' counsel with hearing ears; to ask their advice and to admit to having found it good; to be willing to abide by what they feel is right and best. It is humility that brings willingness to give others credit for all they do, never appropriating for oneself more than is rightfully his. It is humility that makes the child willing to let another, better able than he, take a place that he would like to have, and then to give him generous help and support. No day comes but that a child has need for humility such as this.

It is humility that makes it possible for a child to take praise and commendation without resulting vanity and conceit; to take success without self-exaltation, bragging, and boastfulness; to take the lead among his fellows without arrogant domination. It is only through humility that one can gracefully accept and profit by criticism; that one can honestly admit, "I don't know" with no pretense to knowledge he does not have; that one can accept offered help graciously and use it willingly instead of pushing it aside with proud self-sufficiency.

It takes humility to accord recognition to another's talents and achievements and to rejoice in them; to recognize and defer to greater experience and more knowledge or ability than one's own but with no subservience, self-abasement or deprecatory self-effacement in the deference given. None of these three are ever true humility. They are only a form of egotism parading as humility.

True humility recognizes one's own worth as well as the worth of others. With true humility one accepts his own individuality with the same fair and honest recognition of talents, abilities, qualities, and values held as one accords to another. Nor does true humility mean the withholding of opinions or ideas or the belittling of them. It means only that they shall not be set forth as superior to all others or with the demand that they be unquestionably accepted. Neither does humility mean that there may not rightly be pride in achievement, but only that it shall not be the pride of vainglory or lead one into self-exaltation and self-importance. These are thoughts to help a child to lay hold upon, thoughts that help him in all his relationships, thoughts that help him to get his sights set truly on values that are lasting.

It was some of these thoughts that the parents of eleven-year-old Larry were trying to help him accept when his election as president of his class seemed to be taken with no slight trace of the humility they wanted him to learn. "Nobody else had a chance," he boasted to a younger brother. "They knew there wasn't another kid could do it." Then later to his sister, "Look, Sis, if you want to get elected to something you just watch me and you'll make it." He fairly strutted in his importance.

"Let's think a little, Son," his father said later in the evening after there had been ample rejoicing over the honor received. "Let's think what qualities you have that will make you a good president for the class. You know they have given you quite a responsibility."

"Oh sure," said the boy, "but they knew I could do it."

It took more than one talk before the lad came to see that being given that responsibility was being given an opportunity to serve, to be helpful, to be useful; that this was a chance to think of the whole class and what he could do for them; that the service he gave would be the measure of his success; that there would be many things that different ones could do to help him. It was so that this father helped the boy to a thought a little more humble than he had brought home from school that day.

A humble thought is ever a generous thought ready to give of time, effort, knowledge, comfort, whatever is needed, with gladness to be able to serve. It is a thought that does not demand glory in return but is satisfied with giving.

It was another thought that sixteen-year-old Linda's parents brought to her when she came home all upset over an English assignment which directed that each student write a theme on a self-chosen topic but based on an interview with some prominent person in the community. "I can't do it," said Linda in tears, "I can't do it. Who am I to go to someone prominent? They'd just laugh at me." That was timidity, not humility; timidity with a trace of self-depreciation.

"Who are you?" said Mother. "You are a high school student trying honestly to get the information for an assignment that you want to do conscientiously."

"Who are you?" said Dad. "You are a sixteen-year-old going to someone older who you recognize has more knowledge and experience than you have and asking for the benefit of it."

Together the parents helped the girl to build her confidence until she felt able to arrange for her interview and go to it with dignity, calmness, assurance. Part of that confidence came from the careful thought they helped her give to the topic on which she wanted to work and to the thoughtful selection of the person best qualified to give her the help she needed. It was with a truly humble thought that she went to the interview. She was prepared. It takes a humble thought to make thorough preparation instead of trusting to quickness of wit or pleasantness and charm of manner. She went with self-confidence that came not only from her preparation but from the self-respect the parents helped her feel as a willing learner.

Humility, confidence and self-respect go hand in hand. Confidence gives to humility strength. Humility holds confidence in check, thus preventing its becoming arrogant. Self-respect in turn gives strength to humility, and humility never lets self-respect become self-importance.

It is by thinking thoughts in which humility has its roots that a child learns to live the quality. A humble thought is always a willing, receptive thought, receptive to the truth, open to new, fresh ideas, ready to allow those ideas to unfold and to modify the old in light of the new. That willingness to forego preconceived opinions and beliefs when new insight comes could never be without humility, nor could the willingness to accept understanding from whatever source it may come even though it be from the speech or actions of a little child. In the humble thought, willingness to learn is never hampered because of intellectual attainments, because of position, prestige, titles, awards or honors of any sort. When these come, the one with humble thought accepts them gratefully, uses them wisely, makes of them an opportunity for service, never with the feeling of having reached the pinnacle of success but ever mindful that always beyond lies more to be learned.

It is humility that helps one to hold to the spiritual and moral values that are true and substantial without being deflected from adherence to them by flattery or personal adulation, or tempted to sacrifice them in a feverish reaching out for more elevation of self. Flattery and personal adulation are temptations to children no less than to grown-ups and they, like grown-ups, need the humility that helps them not to become

Teaching Moral and Spiritual Values

so enamored of them as to seek them above all else.

Fourteen-year-old June is a girl with that humility. She is a popular girl liked by boys and girls alike, liked and respected by teachers. She is free and easy with everyone, a good student, active in everything in school, always being elected to something or being given some honor. With it all she never becomes patronizing with others, never sets herself off with any clique, never seems to have any feeling of superiority because of her popularity or achievements. The learning of the humility which has kept her unspoiled did not just happen. It came with thoughtful guidance from the time she was a very little girl, guidance that as her mother told it, kept her from being the show-off she might so easily have been; guidance that kept her from being vain about her looks and conceited about her abilities; guidance that helped her to a friendliness that had in it no play for praise nor any thought of personal gain. Those parents gave her guidance that brought out the true humility without which genuine, heartfelt popularity is never accorded. This it is useful for a child to come to see.

Humility is a foundation stone for respect, respect of children for parents, of parents for children, respect for any individual because he is an individual. Respect is deferential regard, esteem, admiration with honor, and can be given only when humility brings these feelings to the fore without the egotism that would blind one to the qualities in another worthy of one's high regard.

It is through humility that one catches sight of greatness in others, that makes one willing to acknowledge that greatness, that makes one reach out with desire to emulate it. It is through humility that one catches glimpses of great spiritual truths and comes to see them clearly, for it is only through humility that one is willing to open thought that they may be revealed.

It is humility that enables one to look at his motives and see them clearly and truly. It is humility that enables one in the quietness of his own thought to purify and elevate those motives when they are seen to be less worthy than one would have them. It is humility that leads those who acknowledge a Supreme Divine Power to turn to that Power for wisdom and guidance. It takes humility to acknowledge such a Power.

No, humility is never a quality of weakness. It is a quality of great strength, strength that enables one to stand in the face of unkindness, injustice, anger, hatred, and hold serenely to love, kindness and compassion instead of responding with counterattack. Humility has power, all the power that the love, kindness and unselfish, generous thought which are its component parts forever wield.

87

Long before a child can understand all the many facets of humility and all of its usefulness in living, he can come to understand and think the thoughts from which it comes forth. It takes humility, great humility, to teach humility; humility that makes one ready to say to a child "I was wrong," or, "It might have been better for you to do as you wanted to," or, "How does this look to you?" or, "Your ideas were very useful." It takes humility to listen to a child, to accept his ideas, to acknowledge that he has a right to his opinion. It takes humility to be willing to learn from a child, to admit that one has learned.

Humility in a child's bringing-up brings great strength to it. With humility one can set sights on the spiritual and moral qualities one would have him learn. With love and tenderness one can guide him in their learning. With earnestness and sincerity one can strive to live those qualities in his sight. With open-mindedness and eagerness one can welcome into thought any idea helpful to that guidance. With un-selfed interest one can ever seek that which is best for the child. With patience one can correct both his mistakes and one's own.

With gladness one rejoices when there unfolds to view in the child's living the humility that helps him to stand true to principles when hate, anger, greed, will to power, or longing for adulation would tempt him; that humility which brings one ever closer to good, ever more ready to acknowledge it, ever more grateful for it. Humility is a foundation stone for true contentment, for successful accomplishment, for happy harmonious relationships.

8

GRATITUDE

TRUE GRATITUDE is an inner feeling, an innermost thought that wells up with gladsome, joyous thankfulness for good. It is toward this feeling, this thought, that one who would help a child to learn to live the quality of gratitude must give direct attention. It is only out of a grateful feeling and thought that true gratitude can ever come. Without these any words or actions purporting to express it are empty, devoid of the sincerity and genuineness which are its indelible mark.

A child can readily learn to feel the feelings and think the thoughts in which the gratitude that is a spiritual quality has its roots. Frequently he does not so learn, because the help needed for the learning is not forthcoming. The common idea that a child is prone to take for granted whatever of good comes to him often gets in the way of helping him to see it and be glad for it. One does well never to accept any idea that would stand in the way of helping him to let spiritual qualities useful in his living unfold easily and naturally. Rather, it is a service to the child to set aside anything that would hinder helping him to make his own any quality that would enrich his living.

Frequently one hears complaints that as the child gets older, ingratitude marks his thought. This points to the wisdom and rightness of early teaching of those grateful ways of feeling and thinking that one would have expressed in action. It is unfair to a child to do otherwise, for from earliest childhood on, grateful feeling and thinking bring joy, freedom, richness and warmth into the daily living.

A grateful thought is always a joyous thought because it is a thought that is seeing and acknowledging good. It is a freeing thought because it is a thankful thought. Where thankfulness is, in that measure, there is freedom from discontent. It is an enriching thought because it embraces good, and good ever brings with it love and goodwill. In turn it attracts it to itself, thereby enhancing and increasing that which is already in thought. The love that is ever a part of it

92

warms the one who feels the gratitude and all those upon whom it is bestowed.

"I feel so good on the inside of myself," said a four-year-old, hugging her arms around herself and tilting back and forth on her toes, "I feel all fizzy and good inside."

"Do you know, honey, why you feel so good?" Mother asked.

"I guess it's because I'm so glad about that book," came the child's reply.

"Yes," said Mother, "that's part of it, but that isn't all of it."

Then she told the child how it always makes one feel good inside to be grateful for the loving thing another has done. She knew and she wanted the child to know that it was more than the new book which Grandmother had brought that made her feel good inside.

It was the genuine loving gratitude that the child had felt and expressed that made her feel good. Before she had even looked at the book, quick as a flash she had caught Grandmother around the knees in a tight squeeze with a spontaneous, heartwarming, impulsive, "I'm so glad you're my Grandmommie and I love you, I love you."

But one asks, "Was that really gratitude or was it because she was glad to see the grandmother she loved?" It was gratitude. It was a response to a gift, to something loving another had done for her. Gratitude is always a response to good. Tiny though the beginnings of that child's grateful response might be, it had in it the seeds of gratitude. That mother was helping those seeds to grow by naming for the child the feeling she felt. She was bringing the thought of gratitude into the child's awareness. She was lifting spontaneous feeling to conscious thought. She was holding the child's feeling of gratitude up for her to look at, helping her to know it by name so that she might recognize it when she felt or thought it again.

True gratitude is seeing, acknowledging, being glad and thankful for good. Often a child does not acknowledge it or show appreciation for it, because he does not see it. This then points to the teaching that helps him to see it; that opens his eyes to it; that brings it into the focus of his attention; that sets his sights on it. Seeing it, being alert to it, is basically essential to being grateful for it.

"Well," said a father, "it was pretty nice of Mother to do that, wasn't it?" And a child takes note of a thoughtful act, even if only momentarily, that might otherwise have passed unnoticed. He catches a glimpse of the good another is bringing to him. "That was kind of her to go out of her way to give you boys those cookies," says Mother. And the child sees a neighbor's act as more than merely the cookies he liked. "Auntie Sue must have spent a good deal of time making that for you." And the gift becomes the gift plus the thought back of it for the child.

Seeing the good that people do and being grateful for it go beyond what is done for oneself to the good done for others as well. Seeing it is a forward step for a child to take in the recognition of good. Being glad for it is a step toward being glad for all good and not merely for that coming to him individually. There is the good to mention to him that is done for other members of the family, for neighbors, in the community, good deeds recounted in newspapers.

It was one of these that eleven-year-old Henry's Dad called to his attention. The tale was of a dog that needed a home and the great number of people who came forth with offers. It was an interesting and heart-warming story but the lad's father made more than that of it. "You know," he said to the boy, "if you keep your eyes and ears open you can find good everywhere you look."

Such a search is sure to be a fruitful one and richly rewarding to a child who undertakes it. There is the child's home for him to think about, the care and protection of parents, the kindnesses of brothers, sisters and relatives; his school and all its provisions for his learning; the community in which he lives, the protection and advantages it offers; the free way of life under which we live.

Nor need one stop at that which lies immediately at hand. Turn to history and biography and what richness a child can find as one helps him to see the services that individuals have given to help their fellowman throughout the ages; to recognize the thoughts of good that have been set down in prose and poetry in both secular and sacred literature. This is all a part of opening a child's thought to good in order that he may be grateful for it. Without the seeing there cannot be the gratitude which one would have him come to feel and to express.

When there is gratitude in thought it is natural for it to come into expression even though it may be only a fleeting bit of appreciation evidenced in a little child's shy smile and quick happy glance at the giver. There needs must be help for a child to bring his gratitude into expression. Even when he feels it, shyness and timidity may stand in the way of its coming forth. Or he actually does not know what one does or says to show it or, indeed, that it need be shown.

It is not enough to put the words "thank you" into a child's mouth or to prod him into saying them. It is right that he should learn to say them, but only when they come from a grateful feeling. As the feeling comes so can the words that are his own spontaneous expression. "I like it more than anything," said a three-year-old. "It's what I wanted the most and the most of all," said a five-year-old. "How did you think about taking me to the city?" asked an eight-year-old, with unmistakable gratitude for the trip an aunt had planned. All of these were sincere words, spontaneously spoken out of a grateful thought.

But what, one asks, if a gift given or a kindly deed offered is one which the child does not like or want? Shall words of appreciation be spoken when no gratitude is felt? No, but with a little help a child can see through the gift for which he does not care to the thoughtfulness behind the gift and be grateful for that.

Words of genuine gratitude are good to hear and a child can learn to put grateful thoughts into gracious words. Actions, though, forever speak louder than words. This a child can learn as he is helped to see that willing obedience bespeaks gratitude for all that parents do for him as does also his ready giving of help; his cheerful assent to whatever is asked; his thoughtful doing of little acts of kindness; his listening to parents' counsel; his gracious acceptance of their correction.

True gratitude is a strong, powerful spiritual quality. It has back of it all the colorful force of the good which it acknowledges and for which it gives its gladsome thanks. Through speech and action the gratitude one feels goes out to warm and bless all who feel its touch.

As parents seek to teach their children to feel and live gratefully they will, if they believe in a Divine Power as the ultimate source of all good, naturally turn their child's thought in gratitude to that Power. Whatever one's belief, there could scarcely be the teaching of gratitude as a spiritual quality without the teaching of some source of the good the recognition of which is ever the basis for gratitude and which reaches beyond the materialistic and the tangibly evident.

Gratitude like every spiritual quality is intertwined with other qualities, each adding strength to the other and all going into the unfolding of a child's strong, fine character.

Gratitude has in it humility, else self would hide the view of good which is the cause for the gratitude. It takes humility to pour forth gratitude generously to others and to receive and accept it graciously oneself. Often the giving comes more easily than the receiving. Pride in being always the generous giver stands in the way of receiving graciously. Frequently, there is awkwardness and embarrassment in receiving that come from lack of knowing how to do it. "I think Danny liked doing that for you," said a mother, thereby giving timely help to the seven-year-old who was shrinking back from the grateful thanks of a neighbor for whom he had done an errand. His shy smile gave assent to Mother's words and another time he will know better how to accept gratitude as it is offered.

There is honesty in gratitude, else it is not true gratitude. Parents need to be ever sure that there is gratitude in the thought of the child before giving him words to say or suggesting acts to perform with which to express what one hopes he is feeling. Otherwise, it is the letter without the spirit, the form without the substance.

Love is a part of gratitude, the love of good wherever seen, love that reaches out with warm thankfulness for it, with eager willingness to acknowledge it, with sincere desire to show the appreciation of it. It is the love that is an inherent part of it that gives to gratitude its warmth, its kindliness, its gentleness, its serenity, for gratitude is ever gentle and serene. It is love from which gratitude springs and in turn gratitude is love's truest expression. It is a quality in which other spiritual graces find ready root and steady nourishment. It is a quality that parents do well to begin early to help a child to learn.

Gratitude spoken before him to others makes the words that speak it familiar to his ears. Gratitude spoken to him for the obedience he gives, for the thoughtful things he does, for the joy he expresses, sets the example of how he too may bring his gratitude to those around him. Gratitude for all good frequently expressed in his hearing gives him the idea that good is cause for gratitude both for him and for the grown-ups around him. When he lives in the midst of gratitude for all good felt, thought, spoken, brought into action, it brings to him gratitude as a natural way of living and grateful thinking as a natural way of thinking.

9

LOVE

Love is a spiritual quality which gives to every other quality its warmth, gentleness, tenderness, compassion, kindliness, thoughtfulness. It is a strong, vital, virile, active quality. It springs from an abiding consciousness of infinite eternal good, that consciousness which engenders the thought that yearns to enfold all others in the good it knows. Love finds its expression in words and deeds of unfailing and ever present goodwill. Such a love is of the spirit and is all inclusive and all pervasive. It is evident in all the fineness, beauty and beneficence of human love.

As a child feels this warm, tender love in all of his living, he too can learn to feel it and express it and through it come to understand and live that larger

101

love that reaches out to all mankind with its goodwill. Parents who believe in God as Divine All Power, and teach their child to so believe, will teach that "God is love," and that as he loves he is reflecting a Godlike quality. Those who believe differently will bring to their child their highest sense of the love they would have him to feel and live.

Love is a practical, useful quality to help any child to bring into evidence in his character. A child who loves attracts love to himself. Thus his living is enriched. A child who loves is at peace in his relationships with others, for where love is, discord and disharmony cannot long remain. A child who loves is serene within himself because in the measure that love fills his thought, turmoil and unrest can find no place.

As parents delve deeply into the nature of the love which is truly a spiritual quality a myriad of ways will unfold for helping a child to learn to live it, little ways that tie in with all the minutiae of his daily living. It is only as it does so tie in that love can be genuinely practical and useful to him and to those with whom he lives. Otherwise, it is only an abstract word, a beautiful theory. The love that is a spiritual quality can never be abstract or theoretical, for by its very nature of expressing good it must always be active in that expression. The wider the expression the greater the realization of its reality and power in one's life. This a child can come to see.

A loving thought is a child's surest defense against the jealousy, envy and covetousness that would so easily beset him and that brings only unhappiness. "Let's think about all of the love there is for everybody," said a mother to her unhappy seven-year-old, "and then I think you will see that you don't have to worry because Jeanne likes Betty so much. There's enough love for both of you." Then later, "Why don't you think about how much *you* can love both of them?"

That was practical help. When a child's own thought is filled with abundance of love, there can be no thought of the lack of it in others. Children need just this kind of help. A longing to have others like them is very real and very urgent. When they learn that loving attracts, they have learned a sound, constructive way of being attractive. It is natural that they should want to be so and right that they should be. Loving much is the answer, genuine loving that sees others with goodwill; that sees them as loving too; that looks for the abundance and not the lack of good in what they do; that is ready to do loving, thoughtful things even though there be no return. Filling thought with love brings its own peaceful satisfaction. It leaves no room for feeling deprived of the love of

103

others; for feeling that others have more of good; for begrudging them the good that they do have.

A loving thought is ever a generous grateful thought, a thought that rejoices in another's good as well as one's own. Not only has it no room for envy, jealousy or covetousness, but no room either for destructive criticism, which is always unloving. A child can learn that refraining from speaking the criticism is going only halfway. The other half and the most important half is the removing of it from thought, or better still, never allowing it to enter. This it takes help for a child to learn. "Yes, I agree," said a father to a fourteen-year-old, "what he did was out of line, but it is not going to help him any for you to be criticizing. He's got trouble enough as it is and he needs your help a great deal more than he needs your criticism." With that he went on to speak of the way one can think loving thoughts about another without condoning mistakes he has made, and how those loving thoughts are a help and not the hindrance that destructive critical thoughts always are.

It is ever so. As one fills thought with another's mistakes to that extent they become a part of one's own consciousness, and the harm they do is thereby extended rather than stopped. A loving thought always prevents the harm from going further. A loving thought is always a giving thought, a giving that is willing, ready, warm, kind, a giving made rich by the love that gives it impetus.

Genuine love always gives with wisdom that sets another's good as the guide to the giving. True wisdom is in itself a spiritual quality. This it is that makes a loving parent check the impulse to any giving that would weaken instead of strengthen; that would foster dependence instead of encourage independence; that would bind instead of free.

Love that is truly a spiritual quality brings with it wisdom which restrains from the selfish indulgence of a child's every whim; from the condoning of that which should be corrected; from any gratification of one's own selfish desire to gain the child's approval by the giving. These are not truly the expressions of love. They are travesties on it.

Love, to be love, must be both unselfish and unselfed. The human love which is the expression of the spiritual quality of love will never seek to overprotect, to gloss over a child's mistakes, to do his learning for him, or to withhold the discipline that helps him to do it for himself. It takes courage to love a child truly and fully with an unselfed love, courage to be firm when firmness is needed, courage to discipline when one would rather indulge, courage to hold forever steadfastly to the principles one believes to be right.

Love that has its source in Spirit brings courage as

well as wisdom with it. It gives shape and form to discipline. It enables one to love enough to discipline. It lifts thought above the material sense of the moment to that spiritual altitude where the fine true principles in which one believes guide the human sense of love into that action which can bring only the highest good to the child. This is parental love in its finest form.

A child can learn, too, to turn to love as his guide to action. "Is this a loving thing to do?" he can learn to ask himself. "Is this what I would want another to do to me?" he can come to say to himself before he acts. Living love is putting the Golden Rule into action, and even a little child can come to understand the meaning of loving his neighbor as himself.

Little children find it easy to love. Their thought is loving. They respond readily to love. They give it forth freely. They need though to learn how to put it into action; how to put it in place of every other suggestion that would tempt them to thoughts or actions less than loving.

A friend has been unkind. Love forgives and kindness in place of unkindness heads the wound and the friendship is saved. Angry words come to the lips as playmates disagree. It is a loving thought in place of an angry one that lets those words fall back unsaid and soon to be forgotten. Words of dissension are spoken by others. It is the loving reply or the loving silence that drains them of any power to hurt. Suggestions of discontent try to enter thought. It is love which is ever cognizant of good that bars them from entrance.

There is no room for discontent in a thought filled with love nor for feelings of frustration or self-pity. A loving thought is a serene, calm, contented thought because it is free from self-will, hatred and all the discordant suggestions that make for discontent. Here lies the sure cure when apathy, blasé indifference, frustrated rebellion, would seem to attack as young people feel the urge for independence and seek to find their direction and purpose.

The love which is a spiritual quality brushes away all that is petty, for sights are set on the right and true. It turns one aside from the unimportant. It lifts thought above the inconsequential to all that is of lasting worth. It is only if such love is brought to the making of decisions that those decisions can be true and worthy. It is the same whether they be the decisions a child must make in his play with others, or those made in the school organization to which he belongs as he grows, or in the business of which he comes to be a part, or in the home which he sets up with the one of his choice, or in the affairs of the community in which he lives and in the world of which he is a part. It is the spiritual quality of love that alone brings the concern for the common good and the willingness to put that good ahead of all else that insures that decisions made are right, honest and useful.

It is the spiritual quality of love that removes self-interest, personal expediency, and the will to power as determining factors in the decisions that are made. Even before a child grows to his teens he can see that here lies the answer not only to his individual problems but to world problems. Basic decisions that are right, honest and good for all can be based on nothing else but love. It is the only way to individual peace and the only way to world peace.

Helping a child to learn to live love is helping him to take his place as a force for good wherever his living takes him. Let no one say that this is uselessly idealistic or impractically visionary. It is neither. Love has power, all the power of infinite good which is its source, and throughout the ages that power has been proved. It is no idle theory. It is a proved and provable fact. Secular and sacred history are full of instances that attest to it. On every hand one who wishes to see can cite examples where the power of love has prevailed. One who has felt the warmth and glow of a genuine spiritual love has also felt its radiance and its power. This a child can early come to feel and understand as parents seek to teach it to him.

Love and service are always linked, for it is in service that love finds expression whether it be the help offered by a child, the work of a teen-ager on a student council, or the service children see parents giving to church, community and world groups.

A child needs to know that his willing, cheerful obedience expresses love; his thoughtfulness in caring for a pet and the kindness with which he handles it; his readiness to do what is asked of him in the home; his steady good-naturedness; his words of appreciation for things done for him; his playing without quarreling; his loyalty to friends; everything he does in trying to live the good he is taught. He needs to know that love has honesty and integrity in it or it could not be truly love; that it has truthfulness and sincerity in it, and justice; and moral courage in great measure. Indeed, it often takes great moral courage to meet hate with love; to set aside wounded feelings and speak words of kindness; to stand firmly for right without either resentment or caustic comment even though met with disagreement stemming from obvious self-interest.

Teaching a child to feel a spiritual love means teaching him love of good, a love that goes beyond human love of parents and friends, fine as that human love may be and is. Love which is a spiritual quality embraces the human love but transcends it in the love of all good, of principle, of truth, of God. Such love is forever gentle, never harsh. It brings forth the best in one. It lights every relationship with its glow. It lifts thought above the love limited to a few to an all-embracing love. It makes the one who lives it loving, lovable, and loved. It is a love that frees from fear. It is forever kind, compassionate, considerate. It blesses the child who learns to live it and all whom his thought touches.

Living such a love in a child's sight shows it forth to him as a natural way to live. Bringing an understanding of it to him in words helps him to lay hold upon the spiritual values that give the point on which to set his sights. Telling him the ways of living it in all the details of the day gives him the help in bringing it into practical expression. This is leading a child on the only road there is to sure and lasting happiness. Love lived is the only way to that happiness.

10

JOY

Truе joy is of the spirit. It has its source in Spirit. It has little relationship with the so-called joy which is dependent on material things and which looks to materialistic values as its source and to their achievement as its reason for being. Such joy, if indeed it can rightly be called joy, is as ephemeral and fleeting as the material things upon which it is dependent.

Joy which is of the spirit is real and lasting. Not being dependent on material conditions it is uninfluenced by them. It remains steady and constant in face of their fluctuations and vagaries. It is a joy that endures. It is an inner glow, an inner gladness, an inner lilting sense. It has its roots in the abiding and confident consciousness of good as ever present and true, no matter what outward evidence to the contrary may be.

Such a joy can be found and felt only as one turns to spiritual values as the guide to living and as one strives to bring them into expression. These and these only can keep the thought lifted above the materialistic arguments and temptations that would ever suggest that by yielding to them and setting up materialistic values as one's guide, one may find the joy he desires. It can never be so found. True lasting joy in human living is the outward evidence of the joy which is a spiritual quality intertwined with all other spiritual qualities and its expression is a natural accompaniment of their expression.

As fine, true spiritual qualities unfold to the thought receptive to them and are put into action, the joy which is a part of them irradiates thought and comes into outward expression as joy in living. There is no other certain way to find it for oneself and no other certain way to help a child to find it. This is a joy that one feels when selfish interest has been laid aside willingly in loving thought for another; when one has silenced the desire for revenge or retaliation and has put a deed of genuine loving kindness in its place, when envy and jealousy have been wiped out and gratitude and contentment have been brought instead into thought.

112

It is spiritual joy that one feels when forgiving a wrong done by another and doing it so completely and so sincerely that one forgets that he has forgiven and loves even more deeply than before. It is spiritual joy that illumines thought with radiance when one denies self to give of service that others may benefit; when one gives with no thought of return, content only with the opportunity to give; when one freely pours forth gratitude in heartfelt acknowledgment of good that has come into evidence either for oneself or for others; when one arrests any impulse to think or speak less than kindly of another.

Each such act springing from a genuinely loving thought brings its own joy with it. The thought though must be genuinely loving else that is lacking of which the joy is an integral part. Without love there cannot be the joy.

It is spiritual joy that one feels when impatience has been quelled and loving understanding put in its place; when obedience to what one knows is right has triumphed over the temptation to disobedience even though the circumstances are unknown to others; when there has been unswerving loyalty to principle even though that loyalty has brought suffering and hardship. This is a joy that has the support of principle, of good. It is in itself a reflection of good.

Spiritual joy is a joy that rises above sorrow and

cannot be obliterated by it, because its source is in Spirit and in the consciousness of infinite good. Indeed it is oftentimes sorrow and affliction that turn one away from the materialistic values which have seemed all important and toward those spiritual values where there is to be found the pure and lasting joy that endures.

This is a joy that brings with it peace of mind, inner tranquillity, outward serenity, genuine happiness. It is a joy one would have a child learn to feel and live; not through being turned to it by sorrow or hardship but through natural, happy unfolding of spiritual values in his thought and willing expression of them in his living.

Some may ask doubtingly, "Is this not to make a child unduly serious and to take from him that exuberant, spontaneous, bubbling happiness that is so markedly a quality of the pure, childlike thought?" No. It is rather that one would insure his keeping that quality; that one would give him the only sure basis for it; that one would early and surely guide him in those ways of living that will enable him to hold fast to it; that one would so teach him that when the discords and disharmonies of daily living beset him, he has as his own the ways of thinking with which to meet them with joy undimmed by them.

It is not that one would ever wish to make a child

grave, solemn, sedate. It is that one would rather give him the only sure way to be gay, happy, free with a joy that can never be taken away. A child can readily learn that it is genuine, lasting joy that he feels when he has done an honest piece of work willingly, faithfully, and well; when he has gone beyond the call of duty to give more of effort than he was expected to give; when he has met a difficult situation and come off the victor over his own fears; when he has stuck persistently to a task though it may not have been to his liking and no one was insisting that he do it.

He can learn that it is true spiritual joy that he feels when he has been loyal to a friend in face of attack by others; when he has had the courage to stand for what he believes to be right though ridiculed for it; when he has refused to bow to prejudice or be lured into acts of discrimination on the basis of it. As parents bring learning such as this to a child, they are helping him to learn to live with joy.

True joy is ever intertwined with sensitivity to beauty which is in itself a spiritual quality. It is with the eyes of spiritual enjoyment that one thrills to the beauty of sound, form, color, movement. It is with spiritual understanding that one sees beyond the beauty that is tangibly material, to the beauty of thought, the beauty of kindliness in an unselfish act, the beauty of loyalty to friends, the beauty of purity of thought.

As one sees beauty he takes it into thought and it becomes his own, a part of him forever thereafter, enriching and uplifting. Beauty lies all around, waiting to be seen. Sensitivity to it is of the spirit, wholly natural to the childlike thought ever receptive to good and adding always to the joyfulness of that thought.

A child who lives with true spiritual joy such as this is free to be happy, genuinely happy. He has reason to be gay, glad, full of verve and enthusiasm, for his thought is filled with faith, hope, confidence in place of fear, anxiety and apprehension. When suggestions of these appear, the light of the joyful recognition of good which is his can be turned upon them and thereby put them to rout.

Spiritual joy is a practical, useful quality for any child to have. It makes his living gladsome. It attracts others to him. It supports him in time of trial and stress. It crowns his days with peace which is ever true joy's inseparable companion. It is a priceless gift to bring to any child.

IN SUMMARY

MORAL AND SPIRITUAL VALUES ARE A GUIDE FOR USEFUL LIVING

PARENTS who teach their children moral and spiritual values and help them to learn to love them and to live them are giving them that which goes far beyond any material gift they might ever conceive. They are giving them of the real, the lasting, the substantial. They are showing them the way to true happiness. They are guiding them along the one certain way to that unfolding of character which makes for useful, honorable, upright, joyous living.

117

Let no one ever say that the teaching of spiritual and moral values is impractical in a materialistic age. It is never impractical to lay hold upon the real. It is eminently practical.

The more materialistic the age the more urgent the need to turn children to things of more lasting worth, that their lives shall be fully rich, neither bound nor circumscribed by any thought that materialistic comforts alone can of themselves insure their happiness. The more uncertain the future seems to be the more vitally important to give to them those values which can never be taken from them; which are eternally true; which will always be applicable whatever the days and years to come may bring, just as they have been applicable through all the vicissitudes that have beset the generations that are past.

This is not the way of weakness. It is the way of strength. It is strength, not weakness, to return love for hate and good for evil whether it be done by an individual or a nation. It is strength, not weakness, to aid those in want, to bestow help where it will alleviate suffering, to give succor where it will lift thought from despair to courage, where it will put self-respect in place of its lack, and all with no thought of selfish gain.

Spiritual values lived are the free way of life. There is no other way to achieve it. They forever free. They never oppress or enslave. It is spiritual values alone

118

that turn aside personal domination, personal will to power for selfish ends, personal ruthlessness that would disregard the well-being of others in the drive to achieve self-benefiting goals. This is equally true for the child playing in a neighborhood group, for the parent managing the home, for the individual in business, for those concerned with national government or those involved in world affairs.

In times of crisis, individual or national, the answer is ever the same. It is only the spiritual and moral values that can be trusted to provide the guide for action that will be upright, honorable and just. Then it is that the habit of acting in light of the values one holds to be right stands one in good stead. Then it is that the qualities through which those values have come to be expressed hold one steady in faithful, undeviating adherence to them, unswerved by fear of personal harm, undeterred by promise of personal gain, uninfluenced by what seems to be personal expediency.

It is spiritual and moral values envisioned clearly, acknowledged unashamedly, followed fearlessly, that lead in the way of right; and as they are followed, all the strength and power of principle supports that action to which they have given the impetus.

It is the spiritual and moral values to which one holds with deep conviction that enables one to say with courage, "This I believe and this I will defend"

119

and then to stand undauntedly in that defense even though self-sacrifice be the price. No materialistic values can ever produce that courage and stamina, for they have in them no principle with which to produce them, no principle to give them support.

It is spiritual and moral values which any individual needs who would live a worthy and useful life: moral values which guide the human action in ways that are right and honest; spiritual values that lift the thought to the altitude of spiritual understanding from which one can see his actions as the expression of principle and thereby illumined with love, kindliness, thoughtfulness, and forever supported by the principles from which those actions emanate.

In times of material ease and comfort the importance of spiritual and moral values always tends to be dimmed in the complacency of the moment and the enjoyment of the luxuries that seem so deceptively desirable, even necessary. Then comes the awakening—a family emergency, a community disaster, a national crisis. In a moment all the materialistic things that seemed so important and satisfying are swept away. Once again then comes the realization that it is the things of Spirit and these only that are enduring, that can be counted upon to satisfy. It is not that one would decry the material comforts and conveniences, or deny their usefulness and desirability. It is rather that one would put them in their place as of secondary importance to those values of more lasting worth.

Never should the importance of these lasting values be minimized or their teaching delayed. Only a false estimate of the quality of the childlike thought will deceive one into thinking it necessary to wait until a child is older before he can grasp them. In the simple, pure, childlike thought they unfold easily, readily, naturally. In that thought are all the elements for fine, strong, sturdy character needing only nourishment and nurture for their unfoldment. The teaching of spiritual and moral values is that nourishment. The teaching of the qualities that express them is the needed nurture. The daily living in which they eventuate is the expression of good that brings happiness to the individual and to all whom his living touches.

A thought filled with spiritual and moral values has in it no place for hate, envy, jealousy, intolerance, dishonesty, intrigue, greed, avarice, all of which bring only discontent, unhappiness, fear and worry with them, and lack of respect from one's fellows as well as respect for oneself. When these are not in thought, they cannot appear in action. What more practical then than for a child to learn that he can reject such thoughts, that he need never admit them entrance into his consciousness, that he can refuse to let them find lodgment there, that he can think instead those thoughts that put into action bring joy, peace, contentment.

This is the kind of living for which the world has need, the living of individuals who have principles and strive to live by them, who willingly reach out for high spiritual values and openly admit that they hold them of greatest worth; who unashamedly acknowledge their belief in a Divine All Power, if they do so believe, a Power that guides, guards and enfolds in a love that they would express in daily action.

It is individuals with high spiritual and moral values to which they are deeply dedicated who are the strength of any nation. It is these values lived that make the moral fiber of a family, of a community, of a nation. It is these that support leadership and government that is wise, right, just. It is from these that such leadership ever springs.

Any family, community, or nation is only as strong as the individuals who make it up. A nation *is* its individuals and it is their spiritual and moral values that give it the only strength it has. It is these values expressed day by day by individuals, in individual families, in church, in school, in community, in all phases of government, that bring greatness to the individual and thence to the community and nation. There is no other way to achieve it.

Let no parents ever think that the fine spiritual and

moral values which they uphold are of little moment in the affairs of the world, or that the teaching of them to their children is inconsequential in stemming the tide of materialism and turning thought Spiritward. Any such suggestions are wholly false. The individual living of spiritual and moral values is the only way in which materialism ever has or ever can be stemmed. Yesterday, today, tomorrow, the answer is forever the same.

It is the spiritual values held with conviction that have sustained men and women through all of history in times of persecution, that have lifted them to heights of sacrifice, that have made them willing to face death itself rather than betray the principles they held dear. It is spiritual and moral values that forever free the thought and throughout all time have led mankind to reach out for a life of freedom.

It is fine spiritual and moral values that sustain men and women today through their rounds of daily duty. It is these values that enable them to sacrifice with no thought of return, that their children may benefit, neighbors may be aided and persons they never have seen may have needed help. It is these same values that give them courage to stand firmly for free and righteous government in home, community, state, nation, government true to the Christian principles upon which our nation was founded and for which before the whole world it avowedly stands.

Parents it is who have it in their hands to teach those values to their children of which the free way of living is the true and right expression because it is based on respect for the individual and his right to live the true and good as it unfolds in his thought. It is those values taught to children at home by their parents that will bring their own reward in inner serenity and calm, those values that have their source in Spirit and derive their inspiration from it, those values brought to human sight through their expression in true, genuine qualities of character. These children can learn. These it is parents' responsibility and joyous privilege to teach.

Let no parents ever yield to any suggestion of discouragement when they or their children seem less than able to live the high values they envision. Those values must first be so envisioned, else they cannot be lived. Once they are seen, it is striving that brings them into action; and the striving itself is part of the fine, true living one has envisioned. Thus does learning go on for both parents and children as great spiritual and moral truths unfold in thought and come into action, bringing good to all.